-To God my exceeding joy-

- To my family-

Three men on a cross
One man dies one is saved
One rises again

Simply Scripture

By: Chris Parker

A Holy Sword Production

All scriptures used in this book are taken from the King James and New King James versions of the Bible

Published by Holy Sword

ISBN 978-0-615-25912-3

Contents

Loneliness

Do not hide your face from me; do not turn your servant away in anger; you have been my help do not leave me nor forsake me, o God of my salvation. He is the one who goes with you he will not leave you nor forsake you. For he himself has said "I will never leave you nor forsake you." Are not five sparrows sold for two copper coins? And not one of them is forgotten before God, yet in your manifold mercies you did not forsake them in the wilderness. For the needy shall not always be forgotten when my father and my mother forsake me, then the lord will take care of me. For the lord will not cast off his people, nor will he forsake his inheritance. I have been young and now am old; yet I have never seen the righteous forsaken nor his descendents begging bread. For the lord loves justice, and does not forsake his saints; they are preserved forever.

Suffering

For I consider that the sufferings of this present time are not worthy to be compared with the glory which shall be revealed in us. For it is better if it is the will of God, to suffer for doing good than for doing evil For to you it has been granted on behalf of Christ, not only to believe in him but also to suffer for his sake and if one member suffers all the members suffer with it for I will show him how many things he must suffer for my name's sake" so they departed from the presence of the council rejoicing that they were counted worthy to suffer shame for his name. And if children, then heirs of God and joint heirs with Christ if indeed we suffer with him, that we may also be glorified together. for what credit is it if, when you are beaten for your faults, you take if patiently? But when you do good and suffer, if you take it patiently this is commendable before God. Yes, and all who desire to live godly in Christ will suffer persecution choosing rather to suffer affliction with the people of God than to enjoy the passing pleasures of sin Therefore let those who suffer according to the will of God commit their souls to him in doing good, as to a faithful creator. For in that he himself has suffered, being tempted he is able to aid those who are tempted though he was a son, yet he learned obedience by the things which he suffered therefore, since Christ suffered for us in the flesh, arm yourselves also with the same mind for he who has suffered in the flesh has ceased from sin for which I suffer trouble as an evildoer even to the point of chains yet indeed I also count all things loss for the excellence of the knowledge of Christ Jesus my lord for whom I have suffered the loss of all things, and count them as rubbish that I may gain Christ for, in fact we told you before when we were with you that we would suffer tribulation just as it happened and you know, but may the God of all grace who called us to his eternal glory by Christ Jesus, after you have suffered a while perfect, establish, strengthen, and settle you.

Do not fear any of those things which you are about to suffer. Indeed, the devil as about to throw some of you in to prison, that you may be tested, and you will have tribulation ten days. Be faithful unto death and I will give you the crown of life. For I consider that the sufferings of this present time are not worthy to be compared with the glory which shall be revealed in us. For what credit is it if, when you are beaten for your faults, you take if patiently? But when you do good and suffer, if you take it patiently this is commendable before God.

Safety

The fear of man brings a snare but whoever trusts in the lord shall be safe. May the Lord answer you in the day of trouble; May the name of the God of Jacob defend you Like birds flying about, so will the Lord of hosts defend Jerusalem defending he will also deliver it; a father of the fatherless, a defender of widows is God in his holy habitation defend the poor and fatherless the 1st born of the poor will feed, and the needy will lie down in safety and you would be secure, because there is hope: yes you would dig around you, and take your rest in safety let them ever shout for joy because you defend them his place of defense will be the fortress of rocks. The Lord of hosts will defend them hold me up and I shall be safe, and I shall observe your statutes continually and he led them on sagely so that they did not fear.

Hope

He breaks me down on every side, and I am gone my hope he has uprooted like a tree as water wears away stones and as torrents wash away the soil of the earth; so you destroy the hope of man I rise before the dawning of the morning, and cry for help; Where then is my hope? As for my hope, who can see it? I hope in your word for what is our hope, or joy, or crown of rejoicing? Israel hope in the lord; for with the lord there is mercy, and with him is abundant redemption it is good that one should hope and wait quietly for the salvation of the lord . But I do not want you to be ignorant brethren, concerning those who have fallen asleep, lest you sorrow as others who have no hope. For surely there is a hereafter, and your hope will not be cut off be of good courage and he shall strengthen your heart, all who hope in the lord. For you are my hope, lord God; you are my trust from my youth therefore my heart is glad and my glory rejoices; my flesh also will rest in hope now hope does not disappoint because the love of God has been poured out in our hearts by the holy spirit who was given to us.

For we were saved in this hope, but hope that is seen is not hope; for why does one still hope for what he sees but if we hope for what we do not see, we eagerly wait for it with perseverance and now Lord, what do I wait for my hope is in you. return to the stronghold, you prisoners of hope even today I declare that I will restore double to you

Patience

Rest in the lord and wait patiently for Him do not fret because of him who prospers in his way, because of the man that brings wicked schemes to pass But those who wait on the Lord, they shall inherit the earth. All the days of my hard service I will wait till my change comes though it tarries wait for it; because it will surely come. I am weary with my crying, my throat is dry, my eyes fail while I wait for my God but if we hope for what we do not see, we eagerly wait for it with perseverance but those who wait on the Lord shall renew their strength; they shall mount up with wings like eagles they shall run and not be weary they shall walk and not faint wait on the Lord; wait I say on the Lord! It is good that one should hope and wait quietly for the salvation of the Lord be of good courage, and he shall strengthen your heart; these all wait for you that you may give them their food in due season would you wait for them till they were grown?

For we through the spirit eagerly wait for the hope of righteousness by faith then you will know that I am the Lord, for they shall not be ashamed who wait for me wait for the promise of the father which you have heard from me wait on the Lord and keep his way, and he shall exalt you to inherit the land I will wait for the God of my salvation; my God will hear me and I will wait on the Lord.

Humility

Do not set your mind on high things but associate with the humble. Seek the lord all you meek of the earth, who have upheld his justice seek righteousness, seek humility, by humility and the fear of the Lord are riches honor and life. The humble he guides in justice, and the humble he teaches his way. "I dwell in the high and holy place with him who has a contrite and humble spirit to receive the spirit of the humble. I will leave in your midst a meek and humble people, and they shall trust in the name of the Lord." To speak evil of no one to be peaceable, gentle, showing all humility to all men. Better to be of a humble spirit with the lowly than to divide the spoil with the proud because pride goes before destruction, and a haughty spirit before a fall. God resists the proud, but gives grace to the humble Lord you have heard the desire of the humble. So humble yourselves in the sight of the Lord and he will lift you up, he does not forget the cry of the humble.

The Lord lifts up the humble; He casts the wicked down to the ground. My soul shall make its boast In the Lord; the humble shall hear of it and be glad; and you shall remember that the Lord your God led you all the way these many years to humble you and test you to know what was in your heart. Therefore humble yourselves under the mighty hand of God, that he may exalt you in due time.

Deliverance

O wretched man that I am who shall deliver me from this body of sin and death, for many are the afflictions of the righteous, but the Lord delivers him out of them all. Is his hand shortened at all that it cannot redeem? Or has he no power to deliver? Jesus who delivers us from the wrath to come, he shall deliver you in six troubles yea in seven no evil shall touch you. The lord knows how to deliver the Godly out of temptation, and the Lord will deliver me from every evil work and preserve me for his heavenly kingdom, for he shall give his angels charge over me to keep me in all my ways. The lord gives freedom to the prisoners so stand fast therefore in the liberty by which Christ has made us free and do not be entangled again with a yoke of bondage, because who the son sets free is free indeed. The Lord is my rock and my fortress. For I have been young and now am old; yet I have never seen the righteous forsaken nor his seed begging bread. For he has set his love upon me therefore he will deliver me.

Salvation

God has from the beginning chosen you to salvation through sanctification of the spirit and belief of the truth. For the grace of God that bringeth salvation has appeared unto all men. Wherefore lay apart all filthiness and superfluity of naughtiness and receive with meekness the engrafted word which is able to save your souls. Whosoever will save his life shall lose it. What must I do to be saved? Believe on the Lord Jesus Christ. He is the door, if any man enter in by him he shall be saved his salvation is nigh them that fear him so work out your own salvation with fear and trembling for if you confess with your mouth the Lord Jesus and believe in your heart that God raised him from the dead thou shall be saved. He who covers his sins will not prosper, but whoever confesses and forsakes them will have mercy. If we confess our sins he is faithful and just to forgive us our sins and to cleanse us from all unrighteousness for with the heart man believeth unto righteousness and with the mouth confession is made unto salvation. Stand still and see the salvation of the Lord, which he will accomplish for you. Now is the time of God's favor, now is the day of salvation. Choose ye this day whom you will serve. No servant can serve two masters for either he will hate one and love the other, or else he will hold to the one and despise the other, you cannot serve both God and mammon. For God so loved the world that he gave his only begotten son, that whosoever believes in him shall not perish. the thief comes not but for to steal and to kill and to destroy. I am come that they might have life and have it more abundantly; For what is a man profited if he should gain the whole world and lose his soul? Truly in vain is salvation hoped for from the hills, and, salvation is far from the wicked wait for the Lord and he will save you.

Power

Having a form of godliness but denying its power, how have you helped him who is without power? The God of Israel is he who gives strength and power to his people he gave them power over unclean spirits to cast them out and to heal all kinds of sickness and all kinds of disease. For God has not given us a spirit of fear but of power and of love and of a sound mind as his divine power has given to us all things that pertain to life and godliness through the knowledge of him who called us by glory and virtue.

Death and life are in the power of the tongue and no one has power in the day of death but you shall receive power when the Holy Spirit has come upon you. He gives us authority to trample over scorpions, and over the power of the enemy and nothing by any means shall hurt you. You are complete in him who is the head of all principalities and power and what is the exceeding greatness of his power toward us who believe we have this treasure in earthen vessels that the excellence of the power may be of God according to the working of his mighty power God has spoken once, twice I have heard this that power belongs to

God. It is sown in weakness it is raised in power. Finally my brothren who are kept by the power of God through faith for salvation ready to be revealed in the last time be strong in the lord and the power of his might and may the God of hope fill you with all joy and peace in believing that you may abound in hope by the power of the Holy Spirit salvation and glory and honor and power belong to the Lord our God.

Freedom

The cords of the wicked have bound me, but I have not forgotten your law. He who has died has been freed from sin, am I not free? If the son of man makes you free you shall be free indeed. For the law of the spirit of life in Christ Jesus has made me free from the law of sin and death. Now I go bound in the spirit; and whatever you bind on earth will be bound in heaven and whatever you loose on earth will be loosed in heaven. For we wrestle not against flesh and blood, but against principalities, against powers, against the rulers of the darkness of this age, against spiritual hosts of wickedness in heavenly places. Not by might nor by power, but by my spirit, says the Lord of hosts. The Lord is the spirit and where the spirit is there is liberty. Stand fast therefore in the liberty by which Christ has made us free and do not be entangled again with a yoke of bondage. For you brethren have been called to liberty. The law was given through Moses but grace and truth came through Jesus Christ who is the way the truth and the life. You shall know the truth, and the truth shall set you free.

Victory

When you are diminished and brought low through oppression, affliction and sorrow, be sober, be vigilant; because your adversary the devil walks about like a roaring lion, seeking whom he may devour. Do not be overcome by evil, but overcome evil with good, that the triumphing of the wicked is short. And this is our victory that has overcome the world, even our faith.

You are of God, little children, and have overcome them, because He who is in you is greater than he who is in the world, but thanks be to God, who gives us the victory through our lord Jesus Christ. Sing unto the lord a new song; for he has done marvelous things: his right hand, and his holy arm, hath gotten him the victory. For you, Lord, have made me glad through your work. I will triumph in the works of your hands. So the lord brought about a great victory.

Now thanks be to God who always leads us in triumph in Christ, I will sing to the lord, For He has triumphed gloriously! Let us go up at once and take possession, for we are well able to overcome it. In the world you will have tribulation; but be of good cheer, I have overcome the world. For whatever is born of God overcomes the world.

Temperance

Brethren, I count not myself go have apprehended: but this one thing I do forgetting those things which are behind and reaching forth unto those things which are before I press toward the mark for the prize of the high calling of God in Christ Jesus. Know ye not that they which run in a race run all, but one receiveth the prize? So run that ye may obtain. And everyone who competes for the prize is temperate in all things. He that is slow to anger is better than the mighty; and he that ruleth his spirit than he that taketh a city. He that has no rule over his own spirit is like a city that is broken down, and without walls. For the carnal mind is enmity against God; for it is not subject to the law of God, nor indeed can be. Therefore submit to God, resist the devil and he will flee from you now when all things are made subject to him, then the son himself will also be subject to him who put all things under him, that God may be all in all.

Gentleness

What do you want? Shall I come to you with a rod, or in love and a spirit of gentleness? But we were gentle among you just as a nursing mother cherishes her own children. I drew them with gentle cords with bands of love. Love suffers long and is kind. Rather let it be the hidden person of the heart with the incorruptible beauty of a gentle and quiet spirit, which is very precious in the sight of God servants be submissive to your masters with all fear, not only to the good and gentle but also to the harsh he has put down the mighty from their thrones, and exalted the lowly. Let the lowly brother glory in his exaltation and be kind to one another, tenderhearted forgiving one another, even as God in Christ forgave you. Take my yoke upon you and learn of me, for I am gentle and lowly in heart and you will find rest for your souls.

To speak evil of no one, to be peaceable, gentle, showing all humility to all men, for he has regarded the lowly state of his maidservant; let your gentleness be known to all men. The lord is at hand your gentleness has made me great. Let your tender mercies come to me, that I may live let your tender mercies come speedily to meet us, for we have been brought very low. Though the lord is on high, yet he regards the lowly.

Faith

I have fought the good fight, I have finished the race, I have kept the faith but he said to them "why are you so fearful? How is it that you have no faith? "Because of your unbelief; for assuredly I say to you, if you have faith as a mustard seed you will say to this mountain move from here to there and it will move and nothing will be impossible to you. Now faith is the substance of things hoped for and the evidence of things not seen. And the apostles said to the lord, " increase our faith.

So the faith comes by hearing and hearing by the word of God but the word which they heard did not profit them, not being mixed with faith in those who heard it. For in it the righteousness of God is revealed from faith to faith; as it is written "the just shall live by faith." that your faith should not be in the wisdom of men but in the power of God for we walk by faith, not by sight behold the proud, his soul is not upright in him; but the just shall live by his faith. Knowing that the trying of your faith worketh patience. Watch, stand fast in the faith be brave, be strong. Fight the good fight of faith therefore being justified by faith we have peace with God through our lord Jesus Christ let us draw near with a true heart in full assurance of faith. Looking unto Jesus, the author and finisher of our faith holding the mystery of the faith with a pure conscience “O you of little faith, why did you doubt? Do you have faith? Have it to yourself before God”. But let him ask in faith, with no doubting for he who doubts, is like a wave of the sea driven and tossed by the wind. For whatever is not from faith is sin. Thus also, faith by itself if it does not have works is dead. But to him who does not work but believes in him who justifies the ungodly, his faith is accounted for righteousness Therefore it is of faith that it might be according to grace, so that the promise might be sure to all seed. For by grace you have been saved through faith and that not of yourselves it is the gift of God but without faith it is impossible to please Him. Knowing that a man is not justified by the works of the law but by faith in Jesus Christ therefore we conclude that a man is justified by faith apart from the deeds of the law

Goodness

Let love be without dissimulation. Abhor that which is evil; cleave to that which is good. Oh how great is your goodness, which you have laid up for those who fear you, which you have prepared for those who trust in you in the presence of the sons of men I would have lost heart, unless I had believed that I would see the goodness of the lord in the land of the living. Why do you boast in evil, o mighty man? The goodness of God endures continually depart from evil, do good; seek peace, and pursue it for there shall be no reward to the evil man; the evil bow before the good; and the wicked at the gates of the righteous.

Seek good, and not evil, that ye may live: and so the lord, the God of hosts, shall be with you as ye have spoken be not deceived: evil communications corrupt good manners. O my soul you have said to the lord, "you are my Lord, my goodness is nothing apart from you" or do you despise the riches of his goodness, not knowing that the goodness of God leads you to repentance?

For he is the minister of God to thee for good. But if thou do that which is evil, be afraid; for he beareth not the sword in vain.

Depart from evil, do good; and dwell for evermore.

Meekness

Blessed are the meek, for they shall inherit the earth who is wise and understanding among you? Let him show by good conduct that his works are done in the meekness of wisdom. Good and upright is the Lord: therefore will he teach sinners in the way but sanctify the lord God in your hearts, and always be ready to give a defense to everyone who asks you a reason for the hope that is in you with meekness and fear. Seek the lord all you meek of the earth, who have upheld his justice seek righteousness seek humility it may be that you will be hidden in the day of the lord's anger but the meek shall inherit the earth, and shall delight themselves in the abundance of peace For the lord taketh pleasure in his people: he will beautify the meek with salvation. The meek will he guide in judgment: and the meek he will teach his way. Blessed are the meek, for they shall inherit the earth.

Longsuffering

They almost made an end of me on earth, but I did not forsake your precepts for what credit is it if when you are beaten for your faults you take it patiently? But if you do good and suffer, if you take it patiently this is commendable before God. But you o lord are a God full of compassion, and gracious longsuffering and abundant in mercy and truth however for this reason I obtained mercy that in me first Jesus Christ might show all longsuffering as a pattern to those who are going to believe on him for everlasting life. And they have no root in themselves, and so endure only for a time. Afterward, when tribulation or persecution arises for the word's sake immediately they stumble if you endure chastening, God deals with you as sons indeed we count them blessed who endure

Weeping may endure for a night, but joy comes in the morning can your heart endure or can your hands remain strong in the days when I shall deal with you for riches are not forever nor does a crown endure to all generations. You therefore must endure hardship as a good soldier of Jesus Christ and consider that the longsuffering of our lord is salvation and we labor working with our own hands being reviled, we bless; being persecuted, we endure therefore I endure all things for the sake of the elect, that they also may obtain the salvation which is in Christ Jesus with eternal glory. For consider him who endured such hostility from sinners against himself lest you become weary and discouraged in your souls. And you will be hated by all for my name's sake. But he who endures to the end will be saved. And let us run with endurance the race that is set before us with all lowliness and gentleness with longsuffering bearing one another in love strengthened with all might according to his glorious power for all patience and longsuffering with joy blessed is the man who endures temptation and so, after he had patiently endured, he obtained the promise.

Peace

Blessed are the peacemakers, for they shall be called sons of God now the fruit of righteousness is sown in peace by those who make peace Depart from evil and do good; seek peace and pursue it I will give peace in the land and you shall lie down, and none will make you afraid you shall not see the sword nor shall you have famine, but I will give you assured peace in this place my people will dwell in a peaceful habitation, in secure dwellings and in quiet resting places. I will both lie down in peace and sleep; for you alone o lord make me dwell in safety you will keep him in perfect peace whose mind is stayed on you pursue peace with all people and holiness without which no one will see the Lord Peace I leave with you my peace I give to you; not as the world gives do I give to you let not your heart be troubled neither let it be afraid these things I have spoken to you, that in me you may have peace.

And the peace of God which surpasses all understanding will guard your hearts and minds through Christ Jesus the lord lift up his countenance upon you and give you peace therefore having been justified by faith we have peace with God through our Lord Jesus Christ and let the peace of God rule in your hearts to which also you were called in one body; and be ye thankful. Great peace have those who love your law, and nothing causes them to stumble. I am for peace!

Joy

Great is my boldness of speech toward you, great is my boasting on your behalf I am filled with comfort, I am exceedingly joyful in all our tribulation my brethren, count it all joy when you fall into various trials but rejoice to the extent that you partake of Christ's sufferings, that when his glory is revealed you may also be glad with exceeding joy do not sorrow, for the joy of the Lord is your strength. He has no greater joy than to hear that His children walk in truth. Restore to me the joy of your salvation and my soul shall be joyful in the Lord it shall rejoice in his salvation

Weeping may endure for a night, but joy comes in the morning. Yet I will rejoice in the Lord, I will joy in the God of my salvation those who sow in tears shall reap in joy. Therefore with joy you will draw water from the wells of salvation they shall obtain joy and gladness, sorrow and sighing shall flee away. To God my exceeding joy, in your presence is fullness of joy for you are our glory and joy. And your word was to me the joy and rejoicing of my heart "these things I have spoken to you, that my joy may remain in you, and that your joy may be full. For the kingdom of God is not eating and drinking, but righteousness, and peace, and joy in the Holy Spirit and things we write to you that your joy may be full behold, my servants shall sing for joy of heart. Let us shout joyfully to the rock of our salvation shout joyfully before the Lord the king I will greatly rejoice in the lord my soul shall be joyful in my God make a joyful noise to the lord all you lands for you are our glory and joy

Love

Love suffers long and is kind, love does not envy; love does not parade itself is not puffed up; does not behave rudely does not seek its own, is not provoked thinks no evil does not rejoice in iniquity, but rejoices in the truth bears all things, believes all things hopes all things, endures all things love never fails. Oh, love the lord all you his saints for the lord preserves the faithful, and fully repays the proud person this is my commandment that you love one another as I have loved you by this all will know that you are my disciples, if you have love for one another" honor all people love the brotherhood fear God honor the king.

You shall not take vengeance, nor bear any grudge against the children of your people, but you shall love your neighbor as yourself let brotherly love continue do not love the world or the things in the world. If anyone loves the world the love of the father is not in him you shall love the Lord your God with all your heart, with all your soul, and with all your strength. And above all things have ferverent love for one another, "for love will cover a multitude of sins." now the purpose of the commandment is love from a pure heart, from a good conscience and from a sincere faith he loves righteousness and justice

If anyone loves me he will keep my word and my father will love him and we will come to him and make our home with him. "He who has my commandments and keeps them, it is he who loves me. And he who loves me will be loved by my father, and I will love him and manifest myself to him.

For God so loved the world that he gave his only begotten son that whosoever believeth in him shall not perish but have everlasting life. The Lord preserves all who love him, but all the wicked he will destroy.

"But, I say to you, Love your enemies, bless those who curse you, do good to those who spitefully use you and persecute you. For if you love those who love you what reward have you? Love does no harm to a neighbor therefore love is the fulfillment of the law great peace have those who love your law and nothing causes them to stumble. But I know you, that you do not have the love of God in let love be without hypocrisy abhor what is evil cling to what is good

Beloved let us love one another, for love is of God; and everyone who loves is born of God and knows God. There is no fear in love; but perfect love casts out fear because fear involves torment by this we know love, because he laid down his life for us and we also ought to lay down our lives for the brethren

To know the love of Christ which passes knowledge that you may be filled with all the fullness of God and this commandment we have from him; that he who loves God must love his brother also.

Who shall separate us from the love of Christ?

Index

Loneliness

Psalms 27:9, 94:14, 37:28, 37:25, 94:14, 27:10, 9:18 Nehemiah 9:19 Luke 12:6 Hebrews 13:5 Deuteronomy 31:6

Suffering

Romans 8:18, 8:17 1st Peter 3:17, 2:20, 3:15, 4:1, 5:10 Acts 9:16, 5:41 Philemon 1:29
1st Corinthians 12:26 Philippians 3:8 Revelation 2:10
2nd timothy 3:12, 2:9 Hebrews 11:25, 2:18, 5:8
1st Thessalonians 3:4

Safety

Proverbs 29:25 Psalms 20:1, 68:5, 82:3, 5:11, 119:117, 78:53
Isaiah 31:5, 14:30, 33:16
Job 11:12 Zechariah 9:15

Hope

Job 17:15, 19:10, 14:19 Psalms 119:147, 16:9, 130:70, 71:5, 31:24, 39:7 I Thessalonians 2:19
Lamentations 3:26 Zechariah 9:121 Thessalonians 4:13
Proverbs 23:18 Romans 5:5, 8:24, 8:25

Patience

Psalms 37:7, 37:9, 69:3, 27:14, 104:27, 37:34
Job 14:14 Habakkuk 2:3 Romans 8:25
Isaiah 40:31, 49:23, 8:17 Lamentations 3:26

Ruth 1:13 Galatians 5:5 Acts 1:4 Micah 7:7

Humility

Romans 12:16 Zephaniah 2:3, 3:12
Proverbs 22:4, 16:18, 16:19 Psalms 9:12, 10:17, 25:9, 34:2, 147:6 Isaiah 57:15 Titus 3:2 James 4:6, 4:10
Deuteronomy 8:2 1st Peter 5:6

Deliverance

Job 5:19 Romans 7:24 1st Thessalonians 1:10
Galatians 5:1 Psalms 34:19, 91:14, 37:25
John 8:36 Luke 4:10 2nd peter 2:9 2nd Timothy 4:18
Isaiah 50:2 2nd Samuel 22:2 Daniel 3:17

Salvation

Luke 16:13, 9:24 John 3:16, 10:10, 10:9
Matthew 16:26 Jeremiah 3:23 Proverbs 20:22, 28:13
2nd Thessalonians 2:13 Titus 2:11 James 1:21
Acts 16:30, 16:31 Philippians 2:12 Romans 10:9, 10:10 1st John 1:9 Exodus 14:13 Joshua 25:15
Psalms 119:155, 85:9 2nd Corinthians 6:2

Power

2nd Timothy 3:5, 1:7 Job 26:2 Psalms 68:35, 62:11
Matthew 10:1 2nd peter 1:3 Proverbs 18:21 Ecclesiastes 8:8
Acts 1:8 Luke 10:19 Colossians 2:10
Ephesians 1:19, 6:10 2nd Corinthians 4:7
1st Corinthians 15:43 1st peter 1:5 Romans 15:13
Revelation 19:1

Freedom

Romans 6:7, 8:2 1st Corinthians 9:1 John 8:36, 1:17, 14:16, 8:32
Acts 20:22 Matthew 18:18 Psalms 119:61
Ephesians 6:12 Zechariah 4:6 2nd Corinthians 3:1
Galatians 5:1

Victory

II Samuel 23:12 I John 16:33 John 5:4 Num 13:30
Ex 15:1 2 Corinthians 2:14 Ps. 92:4 Psalms 98:2, 107:39 I
Corinthians 15:57 I Peter 5:8 I John 4:4
Job 20:5 Romans 12:21 I Peter 5:8

Temperance

Proverbs 16:32, 25:28 Romans 8:7 James 4:7
1st Corinthians 15:28, 9:24, 9:25 Philippians 3:13, 3:14

Gentleness

Matthew 11:29 Titus 3:2 Luke 1:48, 1:52
Philippians 4:5 Psalms 18:35, 79:8, 119:77, 138:6
I Corinth 4:21 I. Thessalonians 2:7 Hosea 11:4
I Corinthians 13:4 I Peter 2:18, 3:4 James 1:9
Ephesians 4:32

Faith

Romans 10:17, 1:17, 5:1, 14: 22-23, 4:5, 4:16, 3:28
Hebrews 4:2, 11:1, 12:2, 10:22, 11:6,
1st Corinthians 2:5, 16:13 Habakkuk 2:4
2nd Corinthians 5:7 Ephesians 2:8 Galatians 2:16
1st timothy 6:12, 3:9 2nd timothy 4:7 James 1:3, 2:17
Matthew 17:20, 14:31 Mark 4:40 Luke 17:5

Goodness

Psalms 31:19, 27:13, 52:1, 34:14,16:2, 37:27
Proverbs 24:20, 14:19 Amos 5:14 Romans 12:9, 2:4, 13:4 1st Corinthians 15:33

Meekness
Matthew 5:5 James 3:13 Psalms 25:8, 37:11, 149:4, 25:9 1st Peter 3:15 Zephaniah 2:3

Longsuffering
Psalms 119:87, 86:15, 30:5 1st Peter 2:20
1st timothy 1:16 Mark 4:17 Hebrews 12:7, 12:3, 12:1, 6:15
James 5:4, 1:12 Ezekiel 22:14 Proverbs 27:24
2nd Timothy 2:3 2nd Peter 3:15 1st Corinthians 2:12
Matthew 10:22 Ephesians 4:2 Colossians 1:11

Peace
Matthew 5:9 James 3:18 Psalms 34:14, 4:8, 119:165, 120:7
Leviticus 26:6 Jeremiah 14:13 Isaiah 32:18, 26:3 Hebrews 12:14 John 14:27, 16:33
Philippians 4:7 Numbers 26:6 Romans 5:1
Colossians 3:15

JOY
2nd Corinthians 7:4 James 1:2 1st peter 4:13
Nehemiah 8:10 3rd john 1:4 Psalms 51:12, 35:9, 30:5, 126:5, 43:4, 16:11, 95:1, 98:6, 100:1 Habakkuk 3:18
Isaiah 12:3, 65:14, 61:10, 51:11 1st Thessalonians 2:20
Jeremiah 15:16 John 15:11 Romans 14:17
1st John 1:4

Love

1st Corinthians 13:4 Psalms 31:23, 33:5, 145:20, 119:165 John 15:12, 13:35, 14:23, 13:21, 3:16, 5:42, 4:18 1st Peter 2:17, 4:8 Leviticus 18:18 Hebrews 13:1
1st John 2:15, 3:16, 4:7, 4:21 Deuteronomy 6:5
1st Timothy 1:5 Romans 8:35, 12:9, 13:10
Matthew 5:44, 5:46 Ephesians 3:19

About the author

Chris Parker lives with his family in Canton Mi, currently in college for creative writing, and Japanese. Second son to David and Valerie Parker his parents, and spiritual leaders. Has taught the Sunday school at various levels and is vice-president of the youth ministry at New Joy Temple C.O.G.I.C.

Thank you

It is my hope that this book can help you in some way and bring you closer to the love of God in your everyday walk with him. Thank you for your support

---

Contact information:
E:mail-cdpa02@gmail.com